Der vollständige Business-Englisch Lehrmeister

Jenny Smith

© Jenny Smith 2022

Alle Rechte vorbehalten. Kein Teil dieses Buches darf ohne die Erlaubnis des Herausgebers reproduziert oder in irgendeiner Form verteilt werden. Die einzigen Ausnahmen sind kurze Zitate und einige nicht-kommerzielle Nutzungen, die das Urheberrecht erlaubt.

Es wurden alle Anstrengungen unternommen, die Inhalte so korrekt wie möglich zu recherchieren. Sollten dennoch Fehler auftreten, kann der Verlag nicht haftbar gemacht werden. Dieses Buch enthält Kurzgeschichten, Artikel und Sätze, die alle frei erfunden sind und nicht auf der Grundlage echter Ereignisse oder Personen basieren.

Contents

Wie man Business-Englisch meistert 4

Part One: Vocabulary 6

General Business Terms 7

Start Ups 45

Online Business 57

Finance. 74

Part Two: Reading Practice 97

Business Pioneer Profiles: David Konner; Advertising Original. 98

When Businesses Go Bad. 109

In the news again. But is it for the last time? 116

The Good and Bad of Online Business. 120

Investing; it's not magic 128

A rough start, but could this IPO be a winner long term? 134

We have economic growth, but is it the right kind? 138

Is it worth getting a mentor? 144

Entrepreneur Today Magazine: Interview with Susan Hendrix. Founder of '*Social?Media!!.co.luv*' 147

Start with what you know 153

A victim of success? 155

Want to make it big online? 159

Different investing techniques for different market conditions? 163

Honesty About a Broken System? 168

WIE MAN BUSINESS-ENGLISCH MEISTERT

Beachten Sie: Am Ende dieses Buches erhalten Sie Zugang zum Bonuskurs. Bitte beachten Sie, dass Sie ihn von einem PC aus besuchen sollten, nicht von einem iPad oder Handy, da die Tests nur auf dem PC funktionieren.

Ich habe drei Jahre lang ausschließlich Business-Englisch unterrichtet und habe in dieser Zeit vielleicht 20 verschiedene Lehrbücher verwendet. Während einige besser waren als andere lehrten sie prinzipiell alle das gleiche Material. Wer mit dem Buch fertig war, konnte eine Präsentation halten oder einem Meeting beiwohnen, doch ist das alles, worum es in der Geschäftswelt geht? Was ist mit der fortgeschrittenen Sprache, die in Unternehmen weltweit den ganzen Tag gesprochen wird? Es besteht ein großer Unterschied zwischen dem Verständnis von Lehrbuch-Englisch und dem Überleben in einer realen Geschäftssituation.

Dieses Buch wurde geschrieben, um Ihnen beim Übergang vom ‚Textbuch'-Englisch hin zu einem selbstsicheren Gefühl in echten Unternehmenssituationen zu helfen. Wir werden 86 der wichtigsten Wörter und Phrasen aus den Bereichen Business, Startup Unternehmen, Online Unternehmen und Finanzen kennenlernen. Wir bieten deutliche Erklärungen für jedes Wort, eine Übersetzung des Wortes und im Anschluss einen Abschnitt darüber, wie man das Wort richtig verwendet. Für jedes Wort und jede Phrase haben wir außerdem einen Link zu einem Beispiel aus dem ‚echten Leben' angegeben, damit Sie sehen können, wie es in Alltagssituationen verwendet wird. In der zweiten Hälfte des Buches finden sich 14 Leseübungsartikel, welche die Wörter und Phrasen enthalten, die

Sie in der ersten Hälfte des Buches kennengelernt haben. Dies stellt sicher, dass Sie nicht nur wissen, wie man die Vokabeln im Kontext verwendet, sondern wird Ihnen auch dabei helfen, sich an das zu erinnern, was Sie bereits gelernt haben.

Bitte an den Leser. Da ich all meine Bücher selbst veröffentliche, ist es für mich schwierig, sie wie ein großer Verlag zu promoten. Wenn Sie das Gefühl haben, von diesem Buch profitiert zu haben, nehmen Sie sich bitte einen Moment Zeit, um eine Bewertung abzugeben. Je mehr Bewertungen ein Buch hat, umso besser. Es kostet Sie weniger als eine Minute und ich wäre Ihnen ewig dankbar. Bitte scheuen Sie sich also nicht und sagen Sie mir, was Sie denken!

PART ONE: VOCABULARY

GENERAL BUSINESS TERMS

WHAT IS AN 'AD CAMPAIGN'?

Werbekampagne.

This is when a company advertises its products or services. Perhaps it is one type of advertisement but it could be many types, for example magazine, TV and billboards.

Example: *As a businessman I often wonder if advertising actually works. I mean, I spend thousands of dollars on an* **ad campaign** *and of course there is an increase in sales, but is it actually worth all the time and money that I put into it? I think with the advent of social media*, traditional* **ad campaigns** *will become a thing of the past. People will be more likely to buy off you if they trust you. So that's where social media is really great; you can actually build up a relationship with your prospective customers*.*

* Please see the social media chapter.

*A 'prospective customer' is someone who may become a customer in the future.

How to use: Our recent **ad campaign** was really successful and we got a lot of new clients.

What is an 'audit'?

Audit.

This is when the tax office or another outside agency comes into your company to check that your financial records are correct.

Example: *I think that being checked up on by anyone can be stressful, but being **audited** is a different (much higher) level of stress. In my second year of business, my company was **audited** by the tax office. Although all of my books* were above board*, because I was just getting started, there were of course lots of small mistakes. Luckily the **auditor** was pretty helpful and helped me get everything in order. If I could give new businesses some advice, I would recommend that you learn good bookkeeping from the beginning. This will help you out a lot in the future.*

*The 'books' refers to 'bookkeeping' which means *to keep financial records for a company, to make records of a company's financial transactions.*

*'Above board' means *'honest', 'legal'. 'legitimate'.*

How to use: My company was **audited** last year, and everything was fine.

WHAT IS 'BANKRUPTCY'?

Insolvenz.

This is when a company can no longer continue trading because it has serious financial problems. Another common phrase is to say that a company has 'gone under', or that it has 'gone bust'.

Note: A more technical term is to say that a company has gone into 'administration'. This is when the banks etc have to sell off the company's assets in order to get some of their money back.

Example: *Since the recession began in 2008 there has been a wave of **bankruptcies** in my field. You may think that this is good for my business because there is effectively less competition, but actually this is not the case. For example one of my main competitors went **bankrupt** last year and I haven't seen an increase in sales at all. I just think that people aren't buying as much anymore so of course a few companies are going to **go under**.*

How to use 1: There have been more and more **bankruptcies** since the recession started.

How to use 2: That company went **bankrupt** because of bad management.

How to use 3: I heard that ABC company is about to go into **administration**.

How to use 4: That company **went under** as soon as the CEO died.

How to use 5: That company is so disorganized. I wouldn't be surprised if it **goes bust** pretty soon.

WHAT IS A 'BID'?

(An) Gebot.

When you want to employ an outside company to do some work for you, you often invite various companies to 'bid' on the work. They usually write a 'bid' explaining why they would be the best company to do the work.

Note 1: When a company 'bids' on something they often include the price they are willing to do the job for. This is called a 'quote'.

Note 2: Another common use of the word 'bid' is in auctions. If for example you want to buy something on an ebay auction, you will compete with other buyers to purchase the item. Every time you offer a higher price you are 'bidding' on the item.

Example: *When local government needs outside contractors to do work for them they usually <u>put it out to tender</u>. This is when various companies write proposals (or '**bids**') and then submit them to be considered. When all the **bids** are in, the local government workers choose the best **bid**.*

<u>How to use 1:</u> I spent all morning writing the **bid** to win the ABC Company contract.

<u>How to use 2:</u> My company **bid** on the government contract.

<u>How to use 3:</u> My first job was as a **bid** writer for a small charity.

<u>How to use 4:</u> I was **bidding** on a car on ebay. Unfortunately there was a higher **bid** and I lost.

WHAT IS A 'BRICK AND MORTAR BUSINESS'?

stationäres Geschäft.

This is a business that has a real shop or offices. It has a physical location. It is not an 'online business'.

Example: *It's strange how language changes over time. I recently heard this term '**brick and mortar business**'. Because there are so many online businesses nowadays there needs to be a word that describes companies that have an actual location. I think it's a sign of just how much the business world has changed over the past 20 years.*

How to use: I used to have a **brick and mortar business**, but I found that an online business was more profitable.

What is 'capacity'?

Kapazität.

This is the *most* one can do, produce, hold etc. For example if your company can produce 100 items a day, then you have the 'capacity' to produce 100 a day. That is the maximum you can produce. Or if a room can hold a maximum of 20 people, then it has the 'capacity' to hold 20 people.

Example: *As a business owner I think that I will never really be truly happy with how things are going. Even if we are getting tons of orders and we are working to* **capacity** *I will always want more. Once we reach* **capacity***, I always start looking for ways to expand.*

How to use 1: We are working at **capacity** at the moment. We just can't produce any more.

How to use 2: We have the **capacity** to produce more, but we just don't have the orders.

How to use 3: What is the **capacity** of this room?

WHAT IS A 'CONSUMER'?

Ein Konsument.

A 'consumer' is someone who buys things. This is the person who buys and uses the end product.

Example: *When designing new products for the **consumer** I try to think about what I would want. Of course in my everyday life I buy things and in that way I am a **consumer** as well. So I try to get into that mindset. What would I buy? What would make me want to buy?*

How to use 1: The best products are those that are designed with the **consumer** in mind.

How to use 2: There are many people who feel that there is too much **consumerism** in the west.

What is a 'contact'?

(ein Business) Kontakt.

A 'contact' or 'business contact' is someone you know in a certain company or industry.

Example: *I don't care what business you are in, if you don't build up a network of **contacts** you are really missing out. These people may not become direct customers, but it's always beneficial to know lots of people from different fields. You never know what is going to happen in business. So having lots of different **contacts** can be extremely useful in the future.*

How to use 1: I have a few **contacts** in that company.

How to use 2: I have **a contact** in the media, so we can speak to him about getting our company on TV.

WHAT IS A 'CONTRACT'?

Vertrag.

This is a written agreement between two parties. It is often 'legally binding' which means that *by law* you have to do what is agreed on in the contract.

Note: If you *win* a contract, that means that you have gotten a piece of work. You (or your company) have been employed to do a certain piece of work.

Example: *An important principle in business is to always have a written* **contract**. *That way both parties know exactly what is expected of them. So if you hire someone to do something, then it is clear what they are***contracted** *to do. They have to fulfill what is expected of them.*

How to use 1: We had a **contract** with that company to deal with all of their web design work.

How to use 2: In my **employment contract** it says that I should only work 40 hours a week, but I often have to do more than that.

How to use 3: My company won the **contract** to build all of the new houses in that area. It's a $5000000 **contract**.

WHAT IS 'CUSTOMER SERVICE'?

Kundenservice.

This refers to how the staff deal with the customers. If they treat the customer well, then it is *good customer service*. If they treat them badly then it is *bad customer service*.

Example: *I think for me, the number one country for* **customer service** *is Japan. It is extremely professional over there. I've heard that some people find that it doesn't seem genuine because it is more 'professional' than 'friendly' but that doesn't bother me. Perhaps the worst* **customer service** *I've had was in Russia, it seemed like they didn't even want me to be in their shop. That was just after the fall of the iron curtain, so things may have changed since then.*

How to use 1: If a company has bad **customer service** I never buy from them again.

How to use 2: I work in **customer service**.

WHAT IS 'CUTTING-EDGE'?

innovativ.

This is something that is the most advanced in its field as possible.

Example: *We at ABC Company produce the most **cutting edge** technology available in our field. We employ the best researchers from around the world, and give them one goal; push what is possible with technology to the absolute limit.*

How to use 1: This is **cutting-edge** technology, it is the most modern and advanced available anywhere today.

How to use 2: This **cutting-edge** research could help improve human memory by 20%.

How to use 3: This technology is really on the **cutting-edge** of what is possible.

WHAT IS A 'DEALER'?

Händler.

This is a company (or an individual) that buys and sells a certain item. So a 'used car dealer' is someone who buys and then sells used cars. They 'deal' in used cars.

Note: Please be careful with this word. If you just say 'he's a dealer' and not for example 'he's a car dealer' people will think that he is a drug dealer. So to be clear, if you say someone is 'a dealer' that usually means that they are a drug dealer. So please be careful to be clear when using this word.

Example: *That business started off **dealing** in normal supermarket wines. But then as the years went by they started to specialize, and now they are the main **dealer** of collector wines in the UK.*

How to use 1: My brother is an antiques **dealer**.

How to use 2: My brother **deals** in antiques.

WHAT IS 'TO DELEGATE'?

delegieren.

This is when instead of doing everything by yourself you assign certain jobs to other people (usually your employees).

Example: *When I visit failing businesses, the number one problem that I see is that managers or business owners are failing* **to delegate**. *They are just trying to do everything by themselves because they think that no one can do the job as well as them. Of course this is not true, and often if you* **delegate** *the work out, the other person will actually do the job better. This is because they can focus on that one thing rather than trying to do everything else as well.*

How to use 1: As a manager, **delegation** is an important skill to learn

How to use 2: I try to **delegate** as much as possible. Otherwise I just end up exhausting myself.

WHAT IS 'A DELEGATE'?

ein Delegierter, ein Abgeordneter.

A delegate is a person who represents their company or group at a meeting or event.

Example: *Our hotel is very popular for holding corporate events at. Not only do we have excellent meeting rooms but we also have entertainment for the **delegates** in the evenings. I think that for a hotel to be successful as a conference center, it must keep the **delegates** happy and feeling as at home as possible.*

How to use 1: All of the UK **delegates** will be staying at the same hotel and then driving to the event together.

How to use 2: I was part of the UK **delegation** to the 'Language Learners' event in Florida.

What is an 'enterprise'?

ein Unternehmen.

An 'enterprise' is a project of some kind. It can sometimes refer to a (new) company.

Example: *When starting a new **enterprise** it is essential to think about the potential market. Are there enough people who want to buy what you are selling? Why are you starting this **enterprise**, is it for fun or do you actually want to make money? You need to be clear about what you are getting into, because starting a new project is often a lot of work.*

How to use: I'm thinking of starting a new **enterprise**. I'm going to teach people how to self-publish.

WHAT IS 'EXPANSION'?

Expansion.

This is when a company tries to get bigger.

Example: *For new businesses, **expansion** can be a real problem. If they don't **expand** they will not be able to compete with the larger companies. But if they do **expand** then that is a big risk. I think that the best thing to do is to **expand** as slowly as possible and try to not get into debt. That way you will have less chance of running into problems.*

How to use 1: I really want to **expand** my company.

How to use 2: Our company **expanded** too quickly and now we are struggling to survive.

How to use 3: Sometimes **expansion** is not the best idea. Sometimes it can actually bankrupt a company.

WHAT IS A 'FIRM'?

eine Firma.

This is another word for 'company'.

Example: *Our company has used the same law **firm** since we started. They are quite expensive but they know our history so we are pretty comfortable with them now. I doubt that we would change **firms** now.*

How to use: I think that **firm** makes furniture.

WHAT IS A 'FREELANCER'?

Freelancer, , Freiberufler.

This is someone who is self-employed but does jobs for other people. So for example a 'freelance' camera operator, does not work for a particular television channel, they are just employed occasionally to film certain shows.

Example: *I think that when you start off as a **freelancer** the best thing you can do is try to build up contacts. The more contacts you have, the more likely you are to get work. **Freelancing** can obviously be difficult at the beginning, but once you get used to it you will start to enjoy the freedom. You may end up making a lot more money as well.*

How to use: I was a **freelance** journalist for a long time. Then after a while I wanted a more stable job so I started to work full time for the local newspaper.

WHAT IS 'INNOVATION'?

Innovation.

This is when you improve on something that already exists. It is *not* 'invention' which is when you think of something completely new.

Example: *Our company tries to concentrate on **innovation** rather than invention. We try to improve on what is already out there. We take current systems and try to make them better. There may be bigger rewards if you are always inventing, but the risk of failure is greater as well. So we stick with what we are good at, and that's **innovation**.*

How to use 1: There have been some real **innovations** in the mobile/cell phone world recently.

How to use 2: Apple have always had really **innovative** designs.

WHAT IS A 'JOINT VENTURE'?

Arbeitsgemeinschaft.

This is when two companies do a project or release a product together.

Example: *When I started my first company I had a business partner and that didn't go very well. Since then I have avoided 'partners' but that has also limited what my business can do. So I've finally decided to do a **joint venture** with another company in my field. Although I will have to compromise a fair amount, the rewards should be really big.*

How to use: We are going to do a **joint venture** with ABC Company to release a new brand of sunglasses.

WHAT IS 'MANUFACTURING'?

Herstellung.

This means 'to make' something. It usually refers to making *a lot of* something, not just single items.

Example: *Britain used to be famous for* **manufacturing**. *I mean it was the birthplace of the industrial revolution, wasn't it? Until recently we used to* **manufacture** *lots of things, including cars, clothes, furniture etc. Now most things are* **manufactured** *in places like China and then imported to Britain. It's such a shame really.*

How to use 1: We **manufacture** women's clothing.

How to use 2: I have worked in **manufacturing** since I left school.

What is a 'marketing strategy'?

Marketingstrategie.

'Marketing' is how a company advertises its products and services to the customers. So a 'marketing strategy' is a plan (or a certain technique) of how they will advertise to the public.

Example: *That company was seriously failing at one point. They were probably about to go bust. But then they hired a new advertising agency who provided them with an excellent **marketing strategy** and now they are doing really well again. Their products had always been good, they just weren't getting the message out well enough. It's amazing how a change in **marketing strategy** can literally save a company from bankruptcy.*

How to use 1: Our **marketing strategy** was to build a following on facebook and then sell our consultancy services.

How to use 2: It's important to have a detailed **marketing strategy** if you want to succeed.

WHAT IS A 'MARKET SHARE'?

eine Aktie.

This is how much of a certain market your company controls. So if in a certain market 100 units are sold a year, and of that 100 you sell 12 and other companies sell the remaining 88. That means that you have a 12% market share.

Example: *A lot of companies worry about **market share**, but we try not to think about it too much. Of course having a larger **market share** means that we make more money, but we just don't like to focus on it. We just concentrate on producing the best products we possibly can and then if that increases our **market share** then that's great.*

How to use: We have a 60% **market share**, so we are definitely the biggest company in this niche.

What is a 'mentor'?

ein Berater, ein Mentor.

This is someone with more experience than you who guides you through a certain process. For example a 'business mentor' would offer you advice and guidance on how to run a business. It is usually a relationship that lasts quite a long time.

Example: *Most business people will tell you that you need a **mentor**. While it is definitely better to have one, I don't think that it is essential for success. I never had a <u>single</u> **mentor** but just through speaking to lots of people that were experienced in business I was able to get the guidance that I needed. If you can't find a **mentor** then I recommend that you just try to speak to lots of people and read as much as possible and you should get what you are looking for.*

<u>How to use:</u> My **mentor** has helped me learn about marketing and how it is always important to think of the customer first.

WHAT IS A 'MISSION STATEMENT'?

ein Leitbild, eine Firmenphilosophie.

This is a written statement that companies sometimes write to be clear about what their objectives are. They often get their employees to read this statement so that they know what the company's objectives and work ethos is.

Example: *Our company has never really had a **mission statement**. But if I had to define what our goals are, then I would have to say that that it is to 'bring people together through the joy of language learning'.*

How to use: Some employees like **mission statements** because it gives them a clear idea of what they are aiming for.

WHAT ARE 'OVERHEADS'?

Betriebskosten.

These are the ongoing costs of running a business. For example the cost of rent, electricity and staff etc.

Example: *When starting a business, a lot of people just concentrate on how much money is coming in, and forget about what is going out as well. Keeping an eye on your* **overheads** *is essential for business success. Our company personally aims to keep our* **overheads** *at less than 30% of what we generate in income.*

How to use 1: How much are your **overheads** running this restaurant?

How to use 2: I like having an online business because the **overheads** are quite low.

WHAT IS A 'PATENT'?

ein Patent.

This is a document that proves legally that you own the rights to an invention/innovation or product. Other people cannot use your ideas without permission. They usually will have to pay you for using your ideas as well.

Note: When you apply for a patent you 'file for a patent' at the 'patent office'.

Example: *If you have actually invented something then you need to get it **patented** as soon as possible. A **patent** will protect you from having your ideas stolen. You can file for a **patent** at a **patent** office by yourself or get a **patent** lawyer to do it for you.*

How to use 1: I filed for a **patent** for my new invention.

How to use 2: I need to get permission to use some of their **patents** before I can finish making the software.

WHAT IS 'PETTY CASH'?

Barkasse, Portokasse.

This is a small amount of money that is kept in the office to pay for everyday expenses. For example if you need to buy stamps or tea and coffee you could use the petty cash.

Example: *Dear John, thank you for looking after the office while I'm gone. If you need to pay for anything, please just use the **petty cash**, which you will find in a box under my desk. Thanks again.*

How to use: It's always a good idea to have some **petty cash** in the office. This saves your employees using their own money and having to pay them back all the time.

WHAT IS A 'RECESSION'?

eine Rezession.

This is when the economy gets smaller for at least 6 months. The economy doesn't grow.

Note: A 'recovery' is when the economy comes out of recession and starts to grow again.

Example: *Even though officially the **recession** is actually over, many people are still in a lot of financial trouble. The problem is that even though companies may be making money, most ordinary people are on very low wages. Most people are on at least 10% lower wages than they were on **pre-recession**.*

How to use: Britain went into a very serious **recession** in 2008.

WHAT IS 'RETAIL'?

Einzelhandel.

This means 'to sell' something. So if you are 'in retail' that means that you work in a shop of some kind. 'Retail price' is how much something sells for to the public.

Example: *Retail is often a good signal to how well the economy is doing. So if **retail** is doing well, and people are buying lots of stuff then that's a good sign that the economy is doing well. I have been working in **retail** since the 90's and have to say that things have really slowed down recently.*

How to use 1: The **retail** industry in the UK has been in trouble since the recession began.

How to use 2: I used to work in **retail**.

How to use 3: What is the **retail price** of this product?

How to use 4: How much does this **retail** for?

WHAT IS A 'ROI'?

Rentabilität.

This stands for 'return on investment'. For example if you invest £100 on advertising and then make £1000 in sales then that is a good return on your investment.

Example: *The first rule of business is to make money. Therefore never invest in anything that you don't think will have a great **ROI**. Of course it is impossible to exactly predict what your **'return on investment'** will be, but through experience you will begin to learn what works and what doesn't.*

How to use: I only put money into things that have a good ROI.

WHAT IS A 'SHAREHOLDER'?

Aktionär.

This is someone who owns part of a business. They may not work there but they own stocks in the company.

Example: *Unfortunately businesses have become too focused on what the **shareholders** want. Rather than create companies that benefit their employees and their customers, companies tend to treat their employees worse than their **shareholders**. When this changes, then I think that companies will really start to thrive.*

How to use 1: Only the major **shareholders** have any real power over the direction of the company.

How to use 2: All of the management are also **majority shareholders** in the company so they really want the company to succeed.

What is a 'sole trader' or 'sole proprietor'?

Einzelunternehmer.

A sole trader (UK) or sole proprietor (US) is someone who is self-employed. They do not have a direct boss or continuous employer. This is a formal word used to describe what type of business you run.

Example: *Starting a new company can be quite confusing at first, so lots of people just start as* **sole traders**. *The paperwork and tax returns for* **sole traders** *are pretty simple so it's a good way to ease into having a company.*

How to use: I was a **sole trader** for many years but then I got very busy so decided to turn it into a LTD company.

What is a 'transaction'?

Transaktion.

This is when you exchange money for goods. You pay for something, or someone pays you for something.

Example: *Computerization has made record keeping a lot easier. As we do most of our business online, the**transactions** are automatically logged. This makes doing the books very easy.*

How to use: Our company does thousands of **transactions** throughout the day.

WHAT IS 'TURN-OVER'?

Umlauf / Umsatz.

This is the total amount of money that comes into a company through selling products and services etc. It is *not* just the profit, but the whole amount that comes in.

Example: *A big mistake in business is to purely concentrate on **turnover**. Of course it's nice to have a big **turnover**, but what you really want is profit. A company with a huge **turnover** could have very little profit, while a company with a smaller **turnover** could actually have quite a lot of profit.*

How to use 1: Even though we had a big **turnover** last year, we had such high staff costs that we didn't actually make any profit.

How to use 2: People often mistake **turnover** for profit. They are not the same thing.

WHAT IS AN 'UPTURN OR DOWNTURN'?

Kursanstieg /-fall.

This refers to when the economy (or the finances of a company) gets better (an upturn) or worse (a downturn).

Example: *Every time they lower interest rates* there is a small **upturn** in the housing market. Then after a while there is a **downturn** again. I think that by keeping interest rates low they are trying to get the economy started again, but they can't keep doing that forever. Eventually interest rates will have to go up.*

*'Interest rates' are how much it costs to borrow money.

How to use 1: There was an **upturn** in the economy after the new government was elected.

How to use 2: The economy has experienced a real **downturn** and people are really worried about keeping their jobs.

WHAT IS 'WHOLESALE'?

Großhandel.

This is when you (a company) buy a large amount of a product from the manufacturer or supplier for a discount. You then sell the products to your customers for a profit. A 'wholesaler' is the company that sells you the wholesale products.

Example: *If you can get a good **wholesaler** then you are more likely to succeed in retail. Try to get someone with excellent **wholesale** prices and that don't make you order a lot at one time. When you are starting out you need to order in small amounts until you are sure that item will be popular.*

How to use 1: I bought a 100 pieces at **wholesale** prices and then made a 100% profit.

How to use 2: The **wholesaler** said that he could give me 50% off of the retail price.

START UPS

A 'start up' is a new business. This is sometimes used in connection with an experienced entrepreneur but usually it refers to people who this is their first business.

WHAT IS 'ANGEL INVESTING?'

Business Angle Investition.

This is when someone who has some money invests it in a start-up business. They usually get part of the business equity in exchange.

Example: *People often ask me what I think of **angel investing**. That's a difficult question. On the one hand, if the **angel investor** likes your idea they are more likely than a bank to take risks and give you money. But on the other hand, they will then be part owners of the business with you, so they will be able to have some control over your company as well.*

How to use: When we were starting our business we spoke to some **angel investors** but they all wanted too much of our company in exchange.

WHAT IS 'BRANDING'?

Branding.

This when you give your business or product a certain image or style. Perhaps you always use the same colour or logo. When customers see your products, they know that they are from the same company.

Example: *In some industries such as 'fashion' having a distinctive* **brand** *is very important.* **Branding** *can make your company seem more attractive. It is also useful to help you stand out from the crowd so customers remember your products.*

How to use 1: That company has a very distinctive **brand**.

How to use 2: When **branding** our company, we wanted to give it a really modern feel.

WHAT IS A 'BUSINESS PLAN'?

ein Business-Plan.

Before you start a new business you make a 'business plan'. This is a written plan about how you are going to fund and build the business. It also shows how you plan to make money. It is a good way of seeing whether the business is actually possible before you get started.

Example: *In business school they taught us that having a **business plan** is the key to success. While I agree that they are useful, I think that you have to make changes as you go along. If you just stick to your **business plan** and don't take opportunities as they arise you will definitely run into problems in the future.*

How to use 1: Banks always want to see a detailed **business plan** before they will lend you any money.

How to use 2: Even though they are a good idea, I've never actually written a **business plan**. I usually just get started and then see what happens.

WHAT IS 'CASH-FLOW'?

Cashflow.

'Cash-flow' is how much money you have *coming into* the business Vs how much money you have *going out*. If you always have enough money *flowing* into your company that you can buy new stock and pay your employees then you have 'good cash-flow'. However, if you sell lots of products but have to wait a long time to receive payment then you may have 'cash-flow problems'. Especially if you need the money from the sales to keep the business going.

Example: *Our company has always tried to avoid going into debt. However last year we ran into* **cash-flow** *problems and had to take out a bank loan. When our* **cash-flow** *got better we were able to repay the loan pretty easily, but we are much more careful nowadays.*

How to use 1: I love the ebook business as there is good **cash-flow**. You don't have to wait for months to get paid.

How to use 2: When starting a new business you need to look at **cash-flow**. Will you have enough money to keep going for your first few years?

What is an 'entrepreneur'?

ein Unternehmer.

This is someone who starts a new business or enterprise. Someone who likes to start businesses.

Example: *What makes a good **entrepreneur**? I think you need to be willing to fail and then just keep going. To have an **entrepreneurial** attitude you need to be constantly looking for opportunities and be willing to take action.*

How to use 1: I think that I'm a born **entrepreneur**. Ever since I was little, I was always selling things and trying to make money.

How to use 2: I love that **entrepreneurial** spirit. That attitude that you can build something from nothing and make money from it.

How to use 3: **Entrepreneurialism** is something that has to be learnt through trial and error. You can be taught some things, but mostly you just have to learn on your own.

What is a 'minimum viable product'?

MVP

A 'minimum viable product' or 'MVP' is a new product that doesn't have many features. Basically you make a new product quickly and then try to sell it. If it sells then you improve it and add new features. Rather than spending lots of time and money creating something which then doesn't sell very well, you quickly check that it sells, and then spend more time and money on it.

Example: *My first mistake in business was not making a **MVP**. I spent a year making the best product I could think of, but then in the end no one wanted to buy it. Now, I always make sure that I make a **MVP** and then improve on it if people start buying it.*

How to use: I always make a **minimum viable product** first. This saves me a lot of money if I then find that the product is not that popular.

WHAT IS A 'NICHE'?

Nische.

This is a small very specialized market. For example the book you are reading is aimed at the 'business English for intermediate learners' niche.

Example: *The great thing about the internet is that you can sell a **niche** product and still be successful. Before if you had a business in a specific **niche** it was difficult to reach your target market, but now through the internet it is much easier.*

How to use 1: **Niche** markets can be quite profitable if there isn't too much competition.

How to use 2: I think that I've really found my **niche** in the language learning market.

What is 'pivoting'?

Pivotisierung.

This is when you start a business or make a new product, find that it is not that successful, and then change the direction slightly. This is done if you find that the business will not be successful unless you adjust the direction slightly.

Example: *At what point should you give up on a project? I think that if you really believe in something you should not give up too quickly. Instead of abandoning something, you should think about **pivoting** over to something that may be a bit more successful. Then all of your hard work at the beginning would not have been a waste.*

How to use: I started a supplement company for men but then realized that it was better suited for women. So I **pivoted** the company and now we produce health products exclusively for women.

What is a 'product launch'?

Produkteinführung.

This is when you release a new product so that the public can buy it.

Example: *The most stressful time in business is during a **product launch**. There's just so much to think about. After the **launch** you can relax a little, unless of course the product doesn't sell. Then you have to start stressing again!*

How to use 1: We **launched** our new **product** in 2013 and it has been doing pretty well.

How to use 2: I've been really busy getting ready for the **product launch**.

WHAT IS 'SCALING'?

Expandieren.

This is when you make your business or enterprise bigger.

Example: *His business was going quite well but he was obsessed with trying to **scale** it. Of course **scaling** a business means that you have the potential to make more money, but it also means that you take on more risk. In his case he just tried to move too fast and eventually ran into problems. I'm sure he'll be fine in the end, but there is definitely a lesson to be learnt there.*

How to use 1: **Scaling** your business is a risk, but the rewards can be quite big.

How to use 2: I wanted to start a business that would be easy **to scale**.

What is a 'wantrepreneur'?

Möchtegern Unternehmer.

This is a slang term that describes someone who is always talking about starting a business but never takes any action. This is not a very polite term.

Example: *I hate the word 'wantrepreneur' but it does describe a real type of person. They are always talking about starting a business but they never actually do anything. My advice to **wantrepreneurs** is to stop waiting for everything to be perfect and just to get started. Conditions will never be perfect, you just need to be brave and get started.*

How to use: I used to be such a **wantrepreneur.** But in the end I got tired of talking about starting a business and decided that I needed to take some action.

Online Business

What is 'black-hat and white-hat'?

Black-Hat und White-Hat SEO Strategien.

'Black-hat' are SEO* techniques that *are not* allowed by the search engines such as Google. 'White-hat' are techniques that *are* allowed by the search engines.

*Search engine optimization.

Example: *When SEO began as a real industry a lot of companies specialized in* **black hat** *techniques. This helped them give websites 'the edge' over their competition. But as the internet has matured, the search engines such as Google have started to ban* **black hat** *SEO. Now only* **'white hat'** *is allowed. I think this is great because if you want your website to succeed you need to rely on good content and not on tactics.*

How to use 1: If you use **black-hat** techniques you will get your site banned from Google.

How to use 2: I tend to only use **white-hat** SEO techniques.

WHAT IS A 'CONVERSION'?

Umsatz.

A 'conversion' is someone who visits your website and then actually buys something. They *convert* (change) from being a *visitor* to a *buyer*.

Example: *I have worked very hard on my website to try to increase its **conversion** rate. At first only 2% of visitors were **converting**, but I have now got that up to about 4%. If I can increase this even more I will be absolutely delighted.*

How to use 1: It's easy to get traffic to your site, but it's much more difficult to get them to **convert** into paying customers.

How to use 2: The **conversion rate** for my website is about 10%. So if 100 people visit my site, only about 10 of them actually buy anything.

WHAT ARE DIGITAL 'DOWNLOADS'?

Downloads.

This is when you transfer a file such as a document or audio file from a website onto your computer etc.

Example: *I highly recommend that companies start selling **downloads** if possible. It's such a great business, as you don't have to spend time and money actually shipping anything. The customer just buys and then can **download** the product immediately.*

How to use 1: I sell digital **downloads** on my website.

How to use 2: I **downloaded** the software this morning and I'll start using it later today.

WHAT ARE 'EBOOKS'?

eBooks.

These are books that are in a digital format and sold over the internet. You can usually buy the eBook and start reading it immediately on your pc or eBook reader.

Example: *People are often surprised to hear this, but* **eBooks** *are now more popular than paper ones. Not only are they great for the reader but they are also great for the publisher as well. They are a lot cheaper to produce, and you don't have to send them to the customer.*

How to use: **eBooks** are becoming even more popular than regular books recently.

What is 'e-commerce'?

elektronischer Handel.

This is when you sell products over the internet. When you have an online shop.

Note: If you sell *services* over the internet this is not usually referred to as 'e-commerce' but it is similar.

Example: *E-commerce has really advanced over the past 20 years. Now you can pretty much buy anything you want over the internet. The only problem with online shops is that you don't get the human interaction that you would in a traditional shop.*

How to use 1: The advantage of **e-commerce** is that you can sell the products quite cheaply.

How to use 2: I've worked in **e-commerce** for about 10 years now.

WHAT IS A 'FORUM'?

ein Forum.

This is an online platform where people can ask and answer questions and have written conversations. They are good places to make contact with other people with similar interests to you.

Example: *Forums are a great way to get new clients and customers. If someone posts a question that you can answer you may be able to convert them into a paying customer. It's a great place to show your expertise and start getting people interested in what you are doing/selling.*

How to use: If I don't know how to do something I usually just go on a **forum** and ask questions.

WHAT IS AN 'ONLINE PRESENCE'?

Online Präsenz, Onlineauftritt.

This means that your company has a website and/or a page on social media site(s) etc.

Example: *Over the years we have built up quite an **online presence**. This has meant that people can find us quite easily on the internet. We have definitely benefitted from having such a presence, as it's a bit like free advertising.*

How to use: Nowadays it is a absolutely essential for businesses to have an **online presence**.

What is 'organic' website traffic?

natürlicher Webseitenverkehr, organischer Webseitentrafic.

This is traffic (visitors) to your website that you didn't have to pay for. Visitors that found your site naturally (organically), and not through advertising that you paid for.

Example: *People often ask me "should we pay for advertising?" While I think that advertising is important, you should concentrate on getting **organic** traffic to your site first. If then you are still not getting the sales that you want, you should consider 'paid for' traffic to your site.*

How to use: I never use online advertising, I get all of my visitors through **organic traffic**.

WHAT IS 'OUTSOURCING'?

Outsourcing.

This is when you employ someone outside of your company to do pieces of work for you.

Example: *For a small company like mine,* ***outsourcing*** *has helped us grow without the risk of taking on too many permanent staff. We tend to* ***outsource*** *a lot of the tech work to India and the writing to the USA and the UK.*

How to use 1: **Outsourcing** is a great way to get small jobs like 'logos' etc made for you cheaply.

How to use 2: A lot of companies **outsource** to places like China and India.

What is 'passive income'?

passives Einkommen.

This is income that you earn while not actually working. For example if you have a website that you don't do much to, but you earn money from letting people advertise on it, then that is called 'passive income'. Even though you only put effort into it at the beginning, it still earns money for you after you no longer do anything to it.

Example: *A lot of internet marketers want to make **passive income**. This is where they make money when they are not actually working. Maybe they sell downloads on their websites or sell advertising space. There are lots of different methods. The funny thing is that even though the **income** is '**passive**', it actually takes a lot of work to set the whole thing up.*

How to use 1: I earn **passive income** from my websites.

How to use 2: Earning money from rental properties is kind of like **passive income**.

What is 'pay per click'?

Pay per Click, Bezahlung per Click.

This is a type of online advertising. Basically the advertiser only pays if the customer 'clicks' on the advert and then visits the website.

Example: *I don't like to have **pay per click** advertising on my site. This is because I only get paid if someone clicks on the link. This is annoying because if someone doesn't click on the link, I'm advertising the company for free.*

How to use: I like **'pay per click'** advertising because I only pay when a customer is interested in my product.

What is 'S.E.O'?

SEO, Suchmaschinenoptimierung.

'S.E.O' stands for 'search engine optimization'. This is when you do things to make sure that your website becomes popular on Google etc. To do things to help you get more visitors to your website.

Example: *SEO is a completely new industry. I mean 20 years ago it wasn't anything and now there are thousands of companies offering SEO services.*

How to use 1: The best way to do **S.E.O** is to just make sure that you have good content on your website.

How to use 2: **S.E.O** companies help you get more visitors to your website.

What is a 'SERP'?

SERP.

'SERP stands for 'search engine results page'. This is the page that comes up when you search for something in Google etc.

Example: *I personally think that the most important part of SEO is getting a good **SERP** listing. If your **SERP** entry is good, then your website will really stand out from all of the other companies.*

How to use: It's important to make your **SERP** result stand out from the other websites. Make sure that you have a good headline that will catch people's eye.

WHAT IS 'SOCIAL MEDIA'?

Social Media.

These are websites where you can meet new people, connect with old friends or make new contacts. The three most popular sites are 'facebook', 'twitter' and 'linkedin'.

Example: *I think that **social media** offers a real advantage for very small companies or freelancers. They can use**social media** to build a following and then make sales. They don't have to spend lots of money on advertising to compete with the large companies.*

How to use 1: I rarely use **social media**, I'd rather just meet people the old fashioned way.

How to use 2: **Social media** is being used more and more for online marketing.

WHAT IS A 'VIRAL VIDEO'?

bekanntes Video, virales Video.

If a video goes 'viral' online that means that it has suddenly become very popular and people are sharing it with their friends or posting it on blogs etc.

Example: *Usually videos go **viral** on the internet by accident. I don't think that you can actually make a **viral video** on purpose.*

How to use: I was really surprised when my video went **viral**. It has had over 1000,000 hits already.

What is a 'virtual assistant'?

Virtueller Astisstent.

A 'virtual assistant' is someone who works as your assistant but they do it online. They do not work in the same office as you. This is a type of 'outsourcing'; you hire someone outside of your company to do the job of an assistant.

Example: *I tried to have a **virtual assistant** but I found the whole thing too complicated. I need someone near me that I can speak to at a moment's notice. With a **virtual assistant** you need to be so organised. But that's the whole point of an assistant isn't it? To get you organised?!*

How to use 1: I hired a **virtual assistant** to deal with all of the sales enquiries.

How to use 2: I wanted to get a **virtual assistant** but I think it would be too complicated.

WHAT ARE 'WEBSITE ANALYTICS'?

Website Analysen.

These are statistics that show you how well your website is doing. It shows you such things as *how many visitors visit your site*, *how long they spend on your site*, and *what the bounce rate is** etc.

*The 'bounce rate' is the amount of visitors that come to your website and then just leave immediately.

Example: *If you have a business website, then you need* **website analytics**. **Website analytics** *shows you how visitors are interacting with your website. Once you know the behavior of your website visitors, it's easier to sell them things.*

How to use: I use **website analytics** to get a better idea of what my customers are actually interested in.

Finance.

In this section we will look at the world of investing and some of the specialised language that is commonly used. You will need to know this language if you work in finance or read the 'Business News'.

WHAT ARE 'BAILOUTS'?

Notverkauf.

This is when a company gets into financial trouble and they are rescued (usually by the government). This happened in 2008 when the US, European and UK banks were 'bailed out' by their governments after getting into serious financial trouble.

Example: *The thing about the bank **bailouts** that bothered me was that it was all so fast. One moment the banks were failing and then the next the governments were **bailing** them **out**. There was no real discussion, they just did it. I still think that it was a mistake.*

How to use 1: I am completely against bank **bailouts**.

How to use 2: Iceland decided to not **bail out** their banks and their economy is actually doing quite well.

What is a 'broker'?

Broker.

A broker is someone who buys or sells shares for you. Some of them offer advice, while other's just do what you tell them to (this is sometimes called 'execution only'). You can also not use a traditional broker and just buy on an 'online share dealing account' instead.

Example: *Before the internet it was quite usual to have a **broker**. But now that you can buy and sell shares online, having an actual **broker** that does it for you is not as common.*

How to use 1: I need to contact my **broker** to get him to sell my ABC company shares.

How to use 2: I don't really use a **broker** anymore. I just buy and sell on an online share dealing account.

WHAT IS A 'BULL MARKET' OR A 'BEAR MARKET'?

Bärenmarkt.

A 'bull market' is when on average all company shares are going up in price. A 'bear market' is when on average all shares are going down in price.

Example: *It's funny but during the last* **bull market** *everyone was totally* **bullish*,** *even at the end when it was obviously all about to go badly. Now that we are in a* **bear market** *everyone is* **bearish*,** *even though it looks like things are about to get better.*

*'Bullish' means that you think the market or a stock will go up in value.

*'Bearish' means that you think the market or a stock will go down in value.

How to use 1: It's easier to make money during a **bull market** because on average all of the stocks are going up.

How to use 2: I usually 'short*' stocks in a **bear market**.

*See 'short selling'.

What is 'Contrary Investing'?

Contrarian-Investment.

This is when you invest in the opposite direction of everyone else. So if everyone is buying a stock, then you are selling it. This is based on the idea that the 'crowd' is often wrong.

Example: *It is very difficult to be a **contrary investor**. You need to be very sure of yourself. Even when everyone is telling you that you are wrong, you need to stick to your own opinion. But if you get it right, there is a chance that you could make a lot of money.*

How to use 1: I am definitely a **contrary investor**. If my neighbor and everyone around me is buying a stock I usually decide to sell it.

How to use 2: **Contrary investing** can be very a successful technique but you need to be brave to go against the crowd.

What is 'diversification'?

Diversifikation.

This is when you buy stocks in lots of different sectors. So for example you buy in technology, property and finance. This means that you have spread your risk around, so if something goes wrong in one sector you will not lose all of your money.

Example: *People often say that it is important to **diversify** when buying stocks. But is **diversification** that good? Ok it may be safer but you will definitely miss out if a certain stock or sector does really well.*

How to use 1: I like to **diversify** over a few sectors, just to spread the risk.

How to use 2: The problem with a **diversification** strategy is that that it is too safe, so you often miss out on big opportunities.

WHAT ARE 'DIVIDENDS'?

Dividenden.

This when a company pays out a percentage of the profits to the shareholders.

Example: *Stocks that pay **dividends** are usually quite big and stable companies. Also, a lot of people decide to re-invest the **dividends** back into buying more stocks.*

How to use 1: That company pays good **dividends**.

How to use 2: Bigger companies often pay their share holders **dividends**.

WHAT IS 'DOLLAR COST AVERAGING'?

Sparplan.

Dollar cost averaging is when you buy a stock or commodity every month at the same time. You don't worry about the price, you just buy it. This is because the price is constantly going up and down so if you buy consistently throughout the year you will get an average price in the long term. This is easier than always trying to get the lowest price, as it's often impossible to guess.

Example: *Timing the market can be very difficult, especially if you are not a professional stockbroker. The easiest thing to do is to just '**dollar cost average**'. This means that you don't need to try to time your buys because it will all average out in the long run.*

How to use: The price of silver is so volatile* that it's best to '**dollar cost average**' if you want to get the best price in the long term.

*'Volatile' means that the price goes up and down a lot. There are sudden big movements in price.

What is the 'floor' and 'ceiling' of a stock?

Untergrenze. Obergrenze.

When people think that a stock will not go any lower in price, they say that it has reached a 'floor' (support). When they don't think that it will go any higher they say that it has reached a 'ceiling' (resistance).

Example: *That stock has reached a **floor** of $2 and a **ceiling** of $3. It seems to be just bouncing around those two numbers now. So support is at $2 and resistance is at $3.*

How to use 1: There seems to be a **floor** under that stock so now may be a good time to buy it.

How to use 2: That stock seemed to have reached a **ceiling**, so I decided to sell it.

What is 'Front Running'?

Front Running.

This is a crime in most countries. This is where the broker is asked by a client to buy or sell a huge amount of shares. Because the broker knows the price of the share will be affected by such a big action, they then buy or sell some shares for themselves to profit.

Example: *Front running is quite difficult to notice. That's why hardly anyone ever gets caught. It does happen quite a lot though.*

How to use: It turns out that the broker had been **front running** on all his clients' major trades.

What is the 'gold/silver ratio'.

Gold- / Silberverhältnis.

This is basically a comparison of the gold and silver price. How many ounces silver could you buy for the price of an ounce of gold.

Example: *The **gold silver ratio** is interesting, because there is actually more gold above ground than there is silver. This is because silver is used as an industrial metal while gold is usually hoarded.*

How to use: I try to play the **gold silver ratio**. So I sell silver to buy gold or the other way around. It just depends on which one is overpriced or underpriced.

WHAT IS 'INSIDER TRADING'?

Insider Handel.

This is also a crime in most countries. This is where people get information about a share that is not public knowledge and then use that information to profit from it.

Example: *Even though it was clear that there had been some kind of **insider trading**, they couldn't find out exactly what had happened. This meant that no one was actually punished for it.*

How to use: The broker was charged with **insider trading** and will lose his license.

What is an 'IPO'?

Erstemission.

An 'Initial Public Offering' or as it is commonly known, an 'IPO' is when a company's stock is first sold on the stock market.

Example: *I tend not to buy stocks at an **IPO**. This is because I have no idea of what the stock is actually worth. After it has settled down, then I look into buying it.*

How to use: The Google **IPO** was one of the most successful in the history of the stock market.

WHAT IS *GOING* 'LONG'?

Long Position kaufen.

This is when you buy a stock or commodity that you think will go up in value. It is the opposite of being 'short'.

Example: *I went **long** on that stock after I watched an interview with the company CEO and realized that they were a great firm.*

How to use: I'm **long** silver. I think it will go up in value.

WHAT IS A *STOCK* 'PORTFOLIO'?

Aktien Portfolio.

A portfolio is the collection of all of your different stocks. So if you have technology, and mining stocks, then your *portfolio* contains technology and mining stocks.

Example: *I have built up a large **portfolio** of stocks over the years. Some of them are 'buy and hold*' stocks while others I only own for a short period of time.*

*A 'buy and hold' stock is one that you keep for a long time.

How to use: My **portfolio** contains a lot of different types of stocks, but I mostly like companies that pay dividends.

WHAT IS A 'POSITION'?

Position.

If you buy some shares in a certain company, sector or commodity then you have a 'position' in that company etc. For example, if you buy some gold then you have taken a 'position' in the gold market.

Example: *I had quite a large **position** in the 'oil sector'. But I could see that prices were going to come down so I got out. I think that if you are going to take a **position** in any sector you first need to do your research and then keep an eye on the market.*

How to use: I have a small **position** in the technology sector.

What is 'short selling'?

Leerverkäufe.

This is a quite complicated technique. However what it basically means is that you profit when a stock goes down in price. It is usually called 'shorting' a stock.

Note: There is an illegal version of this called 'naked short selling'. This is when you sell shares that you don't actually have.

Example: *Short selling is actually quite difficult to do. However, if you want to **go short** and are a retail investor, the easiest way is to buy 'options' or do 'spread betting'.*

How to use 1: I thought the stock was overvalued so I decided **to short** it.

How to use 2: During a recession **short selling** is easier than going long on a stock.

How to use 3: I'm **short** gold. I think it will go down in value.

What is a 'Stop' and a 'Limit'?

Limitauftrag.

Stop Loss Order.

A 'stop loss order' is when you buy a stock and then set a limit on how much of a loss you are willing to make. So for example, you buy a stock for $5 and think it will go up in price. Unfortunately it starts going down in price. If you put a 'stop' in at $4 then you will automatically sell the stock at that price. If you have no 'stop' then you could keep losing money if the stock continues to go down. This is sometimes called a stop order.

How to use 1: I bought at $4 but put a **stop loss order** at $3.5 so when the stock went down to $1 I didn't actually lose that much.

How to use 2: The stock eventually went down to zero but luckily I was **stopped out** so I didn't lose that much.

Limit Order.

A 'limit order' has two uses.

One) it can be used to set the maximum price you want to pay for a stock.

Two) It can also be used to set how much you want to sell the stock for. So for example if you buy a stock for $5 and set the 'limit' for $7 then the stock will automatically be sold at that price.

How to use 3: I bought at $3 then put a **limit** a limit at $5. Luckily the stock went up and I made a $2 profit on each share.

How to use 4: The price was $20 per share, but I only wanted to pay $19. So I set a **limit order** for $19. If the price goes down a bit, the shares will be automatically bought for me.

WHAT IS 'TRENDING'?

tendiert auf..

When a stock is 'trending' it is moving steadily in the same direction. Some investors 'follow trends' which means that they don't look at the details of the company, they just look at whether the stock is going up or down over a certain period of time and then invest in that direction.

Example: *I don't like research much so I tend to just follow **trends**. I find a stock or a sector that is **trending** in a certain direction and then just buy that. If it looks like the **trend** is going to change direction, then I sell and look for other **trending** stocks.*

How to use 1: I try to just **follow the trends** and then choose stocks that are **trending upwards**.

How to use 2: This stock has been **trending sideways** for a few months but it looks like it will breakout soon.

How to use 3: It's been **trending downwards** for a while so I may short* it.

*Please see 'short selling'.

What is a 'troy ounce'?

Troygewicht.

Precious metals such as gold and silver are often sold in 'troy ounces (oz)'. This is 31.1 grams rather than the 'standard oz' which is only 28.3 grams.

Example: *I find that it is easier to think of gold in grams rather than in **troy ounces**. I know it's tradition to measure precious metals in **troy ounces**, but I just find it confusing.*

How to use 1: I bought 30 **troy ounces** of silver.

How to use 2: I bought 30 **troy oz** of silver.

WHAT IS 'UPSIDE/DOWNSIDE'?

Hoch.

This usually means that the stock has the possibility of going much higher or much lower. For some reason, you think that the stock is under or overvalued and could go a lot further in a certain direction.

Example: *I don't know why but the 'graphine' sector looks totally undervalued, there are a lot of companies with serious **upside** there. Whereas in the 'rare earths' it looks overvalued so there could be some **downside** to the stocks there.*

How to use 1: That stock looked like it was going nowhere then it suddenly broke out to the **upside**.

How to use 2: That stock is very undervalued, it has a lot of **upside**.

How to use 3: That stock is very overvalued, it has a lot of **downside**.

What is 'Value Investing'?

Value-Investing.

This is when you buy a stock because you have had a very good look at the company and feel that the stock is undervalued. You feel that the fundamentals are good and that over time the price of the stock will rise.

Example: *The problem with 'value investing' is that it takes too long. People are too impatient and tend to sell at the first sign of trouble, which causes the stocks to go down in price. I know in the long run they will increase in value, but I just can't stand the wait.*

How to use 1: I am a **value investor**. I look for companies that are undervalued but will perform well over a long period of time.

How to use 2: I like researching companies, so I find that '**value investing**' suits me the best.

Part Two: Reading Practice

Business Pioneer Profiles: David Konner; An Advertising Original.

Part One

When you think about famous films, you immediately think of the actors that appeared in them or the directors that made them. You have some sort of image to place the experience of watching the film within. When you watch an advert on TV or see a poster advertising something, you have no idea of who was behind it (who made it). Even though some advertisements are extremely well made, the most important thing is the product, not the people behind the ad campaign. Even though advertising is an art form in a way, people hate to admit it, and feel that it is 'dirty' in some way. They feel that it is 'art for money' and not for 'artistic expression'.

Words and Phrases:

Advertising campaign (ad campaign).

Comprehension Questions:

Do people often know the names of the people who made a certain advert?

What is the most important thing in an ad campaign?

Why do some people think that advertising is a 'dirty' art form?

Answers:

No, people don't often know the names of the people who made a certain advert.

The product is the most important thing.

Because adverts are made for money.

Part Two

Today's business profile is of someone who you've probably never even heard of, but you would have seen his work everywhere. David Konner left school at 16 and started working in the mail room of ABC Advertising (at the time the biggest ad agency in London). He soon worked his way up through the business and was in charge of the company's major client <u>contracts</u> by the age of 25. It was then that he realized that he really wanted to go it alone and start his own advertising agency. He had a lot of <u>contacts</u> in the industry but he didn't have the money. Luckily an <u>angel investor</u> became interested in the project and offered to fund this new <u>enterprise</u>.

Words and Phrases:

Contracts.

Contacts.

Angel investor.

Enterprise.

Comprehension Questions:

When David was 16, what was the biggest ad agency in London?

What was he in charge of by the age of 25?

When he started his company he didn't have a lot of money. But what did he have a lot of?

Answers:

ABC Advertising was the biggest ad agency at the time.

He was in charge of the company's major contracts.

He had a lot of contacts.

PART THREE

Like with most start-ups, money was a huge problem at the beginning. Even though he did have some funding (from the angel investor) he still needed to be careful. So instead of spending lots of money on offices he just worked out of his house. He also outsourced most of the work and only hired freelancers. He even hired a virtual assistant in order to keep his overheads as low as possible. Because he was able to keep costs down he was able to be very competitive on price when bidding for contracts. He soon had lots of clients and became very busy. After a while he realized that if the company continued to expand then he would have to move the business into proper offices and hire some permanent employees. This is where he began to run into trouble.

Words and Phrases:

A start-up. (This is a new business that has just been 'started').

Angel investors.

Outsourcing.

Freelancer(s).

A virtual assistant .

Overheads.

A bid/to bid on (something).

A contract.

To expand.

Comprehension Questions:

Did he employ permanent employees from the beginning?

How did he keep his 'overheads' low?

If the company continued to expand quickly, what would it have to do?

Answers:

No he didn't. He hired freelancers.

He outsourced most of the work. He hired a virtual assistant.

They would have to hire permanent employees and move into proper offices.

PART FOUR

Basically, instead of following his own business plan and trying to scale the company in a slow and steady manner, he took on too many clients and too many staff members and ran into cash-flow problems. He later said this regarding that experience:

"This was an absolutely ridiculous situation that I'd gotten myself into. I mean I wasn't failing because I wasn't successful enough, quite the opposite. I was failing because I was too successful. I had loads of clients but it was all too sudden. Generally clients don't pay until the end of the project but my employees were expecting to get paid on a monthly basis. So I had a ton of money going out but no money coming in. I actually almost went bankrupt and had to sell my house to make sure that I could pay my employees. But after around six months the money started to pour in and things got better from there on."

Words and Phrases:

A business plan.

To scale (a business).

Cash-flow.

Comprehension Questions:

Did he scale his business up slowly?

Was the problem because he didn't have any clients?

What did he do in order to not go bankrupt?

Answers:

No, he scaled up too quickly.

No, he had lots of clients. He had a cash-flow problem.

He had to sell his house.

Part Five

Once he had gotten through those early problems, he soon established his firm as one of the most respected brands in the advertising world. In fact it was their ability to apply a brand to a company that really made them famous. While before they relied on offering the cheapest service around in order to win new bids, they now no longer had to bid on contracts. Clients who had heard of their excellent reputation were now lining up to hire them. When asked about his secret to building a successful company, he had this to say:

"For us, success came suddenly and it almost killed us. We had an excellent marketing strategy for getting new clients *in* but absolutely no idea of how to actually run a business. We had to learn the hard way. You need to have a solid business plan and then expand slowly. I would recommend that any new entrepreneur should get a mentor. This way you have an experienced business person on your side who can guide you through the rough times.

Also you should really try to concentrate on both innovation and customer service. Usually companies tend to either be great at customer service *or* innovation with their products and services. Rarely do companies get both of these areas right. If you can get both, then that is an absolutely magic combination. People will want your services and enjoy doing business with you. There is no downside for them."

So while it may seem that David Konner was just lucky, this is not the whole truth. He was definitely at the right place at the right time, but his determination to leave the safety of an established company and go it alone is what really led him to success. When failure was almost certain he just kept on pushing through. Now after 30 years of pushing, his company is probably the biggest and most successful advertising agency in the world.

Words and Phrases:

A firm.

Branding. A Brand.

A bid. To bid.

A contract.

A marketing strategy.

A business plan .

An entrepreneur.

A mentor.

Innovation.

To expand.

Customer service.

Innovation .

Comprehension Questions:

At the beginning, did he have to bid on contracts?

Does he think new entrepreneurs should get a mentor?

What does he think is a magic combination for business?

Answers:

Yes he did have to bid on contracts at the beginning.

Yes he does think that entrepreneurs should get a mentor.

He thinks that product/service innovation and customer service is a magic combination.

WHEN BUSINESSES GO BAD.

PART ONE

A lot of people dream of starting their own business. The idea of being your own boss and not having to worry about pleasing other people is a great idea but unfortunately the reality is not always as fun. Even if a business does eventually succeed, it rarely reaches success smoothly; there are always problems along the way. We spoke to 3 small business owners and <u>sole traders</u> and asked them what has caused them the most problems along the way and what they would do differently if they could start again.

Tom Holce. Owner of a small company that makes software for 'Real Estate' companies.

"I always knew that I wanted to start my own company but I had no idea of what I actually wanted to do. So for a few years I just drifted around from job to job. I eventually got a job working in computing and slowly worked my way up. Even though I had no formal training, I seemed to pick up programming very easily. I also studied in the evenings and was able to gain a qualification. Over the course of a few years I gradually got tired of working for that company and soon my old desire to start a company began to return again.

Because I was already good at computer programming I decided to make some kind of software. But I had no idea what <u>niche</u> I should target it at. After a little thought I decided that because the property market was doing well at the time, I would concentrate on making software for real estate companies. The problem was that *I did absolutely no market research* and just made a product that *I thought might be useful*. I never once asked any of the real estate companies what they actually wanted. In the end I spent 6 months making a product that nobody actually wanted! I also spent an absolute fortune on advertising during the product launch; which again was a massive waste of money.

That experience almost bankrupted me, but I refused to quit. I sat down and wrote down what I had done wrong and what I would do differently next time. For my next product I went and spoke to lots of real estate companies and asked them what type of software would make their businesses better. They were all very helpful and helped me pinpoint a few areas where I could make software that would help them. I then chose the idea that I felt represented the best 'return on investment' (ROI). After that, instead of spending loads of time making a perfect product, I just made a minimum viable product. Also when it came to the product launch, instead of spending lots of money on advertising I just rang all of the companies that I had interviewed at the start and asked them if they would like to buy the product. As it was their idea in the first place, a lot of them bought the product immediately. So even though I had a rough start at the beginning I learnt from my mistakes and was able to create a successful business."

Words and Phrases:

A sole trader.

A niche.

A product launch.

A return on investment' (ROI).

A minimum viable product (MVP).

Comprehension Questions:

What niche did he target his software at?

For his second product, did he release a perfect product with lots of different features?

For his second product, how did he do the product launch?

Answers:

He targeted it at the 'real estate' niche.

No, he released a 'minimum viable product'.

He rang companies that he had interviewed earlier in the process of developing the product.

Part Two

Susan Star. Owner of an online 'Ethical Cosmetics' shop.

"My business was born out of need. I had been a vegetarian for many years and had always avoided all products that had been tested on animals. Generally it was pretty easy but the one thing I found difficult was finding very high quality cosmetics that didn't contain animal products and were not tested on animals. Over the years I searched around and found a few companies who were <u>manufacturing</u> these products. But I couldn't find a shop where I could buy all of these products from. Of course there were retailers selling individual products but nowhere selling everything in one place.

As quite a few of my friends said that they would be interested in buying these products as well, I rang all the <u>manufacturers</u> and asked them if I could buy their products at <u>wholesale</u> prices. At first I just sold to my friends, and things went really well. Then I decided to start a shop. This was my first mistake.

The problem with starting a <u>brick and mortar business</u> is that you are fixed in one location. So if you have a shop you are dependent on the people walking past to come in and buy things. Even though I did get some passing trade, it wasn't enough to make a real profit. It was at this point that the internet and <u>e-commerce</u> were becoming popular and a friend of mine suggested that I open an online shop. It turned out that there were a lot of people interested in my products, they just didn't live anywhere near me! That's the great thing about an online business, you don't just have to rely on the people who live near you to be your customers. It's much easier to reach <u>consumers</u> that are interested in your specific products. Ever since we went online the business has been growing. Eventually we decided that it was not worth having a real shop so we do all of our business online now."

Words and Phrases:

Manufacturing. A manufacturer.

Wholesale.

Brick and mortar business.

E-commerce.

A consumer.

Comprehension Questions:

Were there any companies manufacturing cosmetics which were not using animal products or testing?

Did she start a shop immediately?

Does she still have a 'brick and mortar' shop?

Answers:

Yes there were some companies manufacturing these products.

No she didn't start a shop immediately. At first she just sold to friends.

No, she only has an online shop now.

Part Three

Jose Lopez. Owner of a Spanish food <u>manufacturer</u> in the UK.

"Although I have lived in the UK for the past 20 years, I still feel that I am very much Spanish. When I first moved here the two things that bothered me the most were the food and the weather. After a few years I got used to the weather and I also found a few good Spanish restaurants. But of course it was too expensive to eat out in restaurants all of the time so I tried to buy the ingredients in the supermarkets and cook at home. As I could only find really expensive imported stuff I decided to try to start my own company and <u>manufacture</u> authentic Spanish food in the UK.

The problem was, that I had absolutely no idea what I was doing! At first I did absolutely everything myself because I couldn't afford to employ staff. But once the company started to grow I took on a few employees. The problem was that even though I had these employees I continued to try to do everything myself. I was terrible at <u>delegation</u>. Another problem was that I didn't know the difference between profit and <u>turnover</u>. So for example the company would make a £1000 and I would just treat that like it was profit, even though I still needed to pay for all the <u>overheads</u> and staff costs before I actually saw any real profit. After about 2 years of making mistake after mistake I finally learnt how <u>to delegate</u> and started to rely on my staff's expertise more. I also hired a book-keeper who took care of all of the finances. If I were to do it all again I think that I would *not* try and do everything on my own. Not only does it drive you crazy it's a terrible way to do business."

Words and Phrases:

To manufacture.

Delegation. To delegate.

Turnover.

Overheads.

Comprehension Questions:

Why did he decide to manufacture Spanish food in the UK?

When he got some employees, did he work less?

Does he still deal with the company finances himself?

Answers:

Because there were only expensive imported products available at the time.

No, he still tried to do everything himself.

No, his book-keeper deals with the finances now.

IN THE NEWS AGAIN. BUT IS IT FOR THE LAST TIME?

PART ONE

This week one company has dominated the news again. It seems that NaniTECH3 are in trouble again. Ever since the <u>recession</u> five years ago, they seem to have had endless problems. The company, which is famous for its <u>cutting edge</u> technology, has slowly been losing its <u>market share</u> to smaller rival companies who are better equipped to survive these troubled times. In fact their only real success recently has been their <u>patented</u> smart phone technology which is a <u>joint venture</u> with a much smaller technology firm.

Words and Phrases:

A recession.

Cutting edge.

A market share.

A patent.

A joint venture.

Comprehension Questions:

When did this company's troubles begin?

What is this company famous for?

What technology do they hold a patent for with another company?

Answers:

Their troubles began 5 years ago. Since the recession.

They are famous for making cutting edge technology.

They (with another company) hold a patent for some smart phone technology.

Part Two

This week there have been rumors that their financial situation has finally got so bad that it is unfixable. Most of these rumors are down to the fact that the company was recently audited and the results are due to be released soon. A lot of the shareholders are worried and have started to sell their shares. This panic has caused sales in their products to drop drastically within the past few months. One report said that some of their factories are working at half capacity because the orders have just dried up.

When asked about the company's future, a delegate at a recent technology fair said that the rumors are not true and that the downturn in the company's business has been caused by mindless panic over rumors rather than fact. Whatever the cause, they will be lucky to survive this week as their share price looks like it has just jumped off of a cliff.

Words and Phrases:

An audit.

A shareholder.

Capacity.

A delegate.

Comprehension Questions:

Why are the shareholders worried?

Are the factories busy?

According to the delegate, are the rumors true?

Answers:

Because the results of the company audit may be bad.

No, they are working at half capacity.

No, they say that the rumors are not true.

The Good and Bad of Online Business.

Part One

There is no doubt that the internet has changed our world completely. Social media has changed the way we interact with each other, online dating has changed the way we meet our partners, online banking has changed the way we do transactions. One of the main ways that the internet has changed our world is through the way we do business. Through e-commerce we can now purchase items at a click of a button. We are also able to hire online coaches to help teach us hundreds of different topics via video conferencing. The list of goods and services that we can now purchase online is endless.

Words and Phrases:

Social media.

A transaction.

E-commerce.

Comprehension Questions:

What has social media changed in the world?

How can you have a coaching session online?

Answers:

Social media has changed the way we interact with each other.

You can have a coaching session via video conferencing.

Part Two

Not only has the internet made it easier for the consumer, it is now much easier to start a company. Years ago if someone wanted to start a business they would have needed much more money to get started. For example, if you wanted to deal in phone accessories you would have had to hire a shop and then sell to your local area. However, nowadays you could run such a dealership from your house. All you would need is internet access, an online shop, some petty cash and a room to store the goods in. While this is great and has opened opportunity up to a greater amount of people it has also given birth to a new breed of entrepreneur. A 'wantrepreneur' is someone who talks about starting a business or does things like writing 'mission statements' or thinks about the 'logo design' but never really takes any concrete steps to actually 'do business'.

Words and Phrases:

A consumer.

Petty cash.

A wantrepreneur.

A mission statement.

Comprehension Questions:

Nowadays what would you need to start a phone accessory dealership?

What types of things do 'wantrepreneurs' do?

Answers:

All you would need is internet access, an online shop, some petty cash and a room to store the goods in.

They write 'mission statements' and think about 'logo designs' but rarely actually do any real business.

Part Three

The internet has also created totally new industries such as <u>Search Engine Optimization (SEO)</u>. SEO is particularly interesting, because unlike 'online shops' or 'online dating sites' it is not an evolution from what was there before, it is actually 100% new. What SEO professionals do is help improve a company's <u>online presence</u>. Basically if you have a website, they help it become more popular. There are two types of SEO, '<u>black hat</u>' which are tactics that the search engines such as Google don't like, and '<u>white hat</u>' which are tactics that they do like. What they do is stuff like make your <u>SERP</u> result more attractive so you get more <u>organic traffic</u>. They also run <u>pay-per-click</u> campaigns to get more people to your website. A good way to make sure that the SEO is working is by checking a '<u>website analytics</u> tool'. This shows you how many visitors are on your site and how they found it.

Words and Phrases:

Search Engine Optimization (SEO).

Online presence.

Black hat/White hat (SEO tactics).

Search Engine Results Page (SERP).

Organic traffic.

Pay-per-click.

Website analytics.

Comprehension Questions:

What type of SEO tactics do search engines such as Google dislike?

What is one way they help get a website more organic traffic?

What is a good tool for checking to see if your SEO is working?

Answers:

They dislike 'black hat' SEO tactics.

By having a good SERP result.

Website analytics is a good tool for checking to see how well your SEO is working.

Part Four

Another popular online business model is something called 'passive income'. What this means is that you are still earning money even at times when you are not working. There are lots of different ways of doing this. One is by selling digital downloads such as eBooks. Once you have written the book and set the online shop up, you don't need to actually do anything; it's all automatic. Another way is to do 'affiliate marketing'. This is when you advertise a product on your website and if someone clicks on the advert and actually buys it (what is known as a 'conversion') then you receive a commission. You could also start a forum or make videos and advertise on them. If the forum becomes popular or one of your videos goes viral, then this can be an excellent source of income.

Words and Phrases:

Passive income.

Digital downloads.

eBooks.

A conversion.

Viral Video.

Comprehension Question:

What are three types of 'passive income'?

Answer:

Selling digital downloads, affiliate marketing, or selling advertising on your forum or videos.

INVESTING; IT'S NOT MAGIC

PART ONE

What is the one thing that impacts our lives no matter how rich, poor, old, young, sick, healthy you are? Yes that's right, it's money. Money is an essential aspect of everyday life but few of us even stop to consider how it actually works. Where is it created? Who controls it? Another aspect of money that most people know very little about is investing. Believe it or not but the movements of the stock market have a direct influence on your everyday life. When for example traders <u>speculate</u> on the price of wheat, they actually change the price it will cost you for a loaf of bread. Also, everyone seems to accept that the bank <u>bailouts</u> were necessary, but how can you say that if you have no idea how the world of finance and investing actually works.

Learning the fundamentals of investing is actually essential for building a secure future for yourself. If you just leave your money in the bank it will be eroded away inflation so you need a way of actively managing it yourself. This is why I think that investing should be taught in schools. Now I'm not suggesting that school children learn how to '<u>go long</u>' or '<u>short</u>' a stock but I do think that they would benefit from learning some of the basics.

<u>Words and Phrases:</u>

Speculation. To speculate.

Bailouts.

To go long. To be long (a stock etc).

To short. To be short (a stock etc).

Comprehension Questions:

Does the actions of traders affect your everyday life?

Does the author think that investing should be taught in schools.

Answers:

Yes. For example if traders speculate on the price of wheat, that can actually change the price of wheat. So the price of bread will change.

Yes. The author thinks that investing should be taught in schools.

Part Two

The first thing I think people should learn about is the difference between a <u>bull and bear market</u>. This would help people to understand that the economy is not always flat but that things go up and down in value. I think that this would help stop people taking on too much risk just before the economy is obviously headed into a difficult patch.

Another thing that would be useful for people to know about is the different types of investing. For example '<u>value investing</u>' would be great for people who enjoy researching companies, '<u>trend following</u>' would be great for people who are good at spotting patterns, and '<u>contrary investing</u>' is suitable for people who are good at predicting changes. If people were taught about the different investing techniques they would feel more comfortable about managing their own finances.

<u>Words and Phrases:</u>

A bull/bear market.

Value investing.

Trend (following).

Contrary investing.

<u>Comprehension Questions:</u>

Why should people learn about bull and bear markets?

Who is 'value investing' suitable for?

Answers:

So they know that the economy is not always flat. So they know when not to take on too much risk.

Value investing is suitable for people who enjoy researching companies.

Part Three

Also I think that people should be taught about 'diversification' (this is when you buy lots of different stocks). This can be a good idea because if something goes wrong with one of your stocks then all of the rest are still ok. Another useful technique is 'dollar cost averaging' (this is when you buy a stock slowly over a long period of time). This is a good method of buying stocks because over time you tend to get the average price.

I think that by learning the basics of investing, people would feel more in control. Even if they hired a broker or a financial advisor to make the decisions for them, at least they would understand what is going on.

Words and Phrases:

Diversification.

Dollar cost averaging.

A broker.

Comprehension Questions:

What two investing techniques are mentioned above?

What is good about 'dollar cost averaging'?

Answers:

'Diversification' and 'dollar cost averaging'.

With 'dollar cost averaging' you tend to pay an average price.

A ROUGH START, BUT COULD THIS IPO BE A WINNER LONG TERM?

PART ONE

An Initial Public Offering (IPO) is always a stressful time for companies, but for ABCD Industries it's been worse than usual. On the day of their IPO there were already allegations of insider trading. Then a month after the IPO a broker was accused (by a famous financial website) of front running a large sale of stock by their client. Even though there has been a lot of volatility (mostly caused by all of the scandals) a lot of analysts still feel there is a lot of upside to the stock. In fact Karl Trombier the famous billionaire investor is reported to hold a large position in the stock. When asked about this he just said that he refused to discuss his stock portfolio in public.

Words and Phrases:

An initial public offering (IPO).

Insider trading.

A broker.

Front running.

Upside (to a stock).

A position (in a stock).

A stock portfolio.

Comprehension Questions:

What were the two scandals that have hit this company recently?

Which famous investor is reported to hold a large position in this stock?

Answers:

There have been accusations of 'insider trading' and 'front running'.

Karl Trombier is said to hold a large position in this stock.

Part Two

Since the IPO two months ago the stock seems to have found a floor at $5 and a ceiling at $5.50. This seems quite stable. But in my opinion, because the stock is so new and there have been so many problems in such a short space of time, potential investors should proceed with caution. I recommend setting a <u>stop</u> at $4.75 to protect you from any potential <u>downside</u>. Also, as the stock has been bouncing between $5 and $5.50 you could buy at $5 and then set a <u>limit</u> for $5.45 so that you lock in your profits. However, if you didn't want to actively trade the stock you could just buy and hold it, as it is paying a small <u>dividend</u>.

Whatever you do, I definitely feel that this is a stock to watch. It's been exciting so far and I imagine it will continue to cause interest in the future.

<u>Words and Phrases:</u>

A floor.

A ceiling.

A stop.

Downside (to a stock).

A limit.

Dividend.

Comprehension Questions:

Where would be a good place to put 'a stop'?

If you didn't want to actively trade the stock, how could you make money from it?

Answers:

$4.75 would be a good place to put 'a stop'.

You could just hold it and collect a small dividend.

We have economic growth, but is it the right kind?

Part One

The government announced that for the first time since the <u>downturn</u> in the economy two years ago there has been growth in some sectors. While an <u>upturn</u> in any part of the economy is good news (we all want to get out of this <u>recession</u>), you have to look carefully at the details to get the full picture of where the economy (and indeed this country) is heading. The sectors which are actually growing are all in the 'service sector'. That means that there are new jobs in <u>customer service</u> such as in retail or working in coffee shops. That's good news right? That means that people are spending money right? Well in a way it is good news but if you look at the other sectors, the picture actually becomes quite scary.

Words and Phrases:

A downturn (in the economy etc).

An upturn (in the economy etc).

A recession.

Customer service.

Comprehension Question:

In what sector has there been a recent upturn?

Answer:

There has been an upturn in the service sector.

Part Two

When you look at some of the other sectors such as manufacturing, design and IT (information technology) the picture is pretty horrible. All of these sectors are shrinking. With manufacturing, almost everything is being made abroad in China or in other countries where the staff costs are lower. It's the same with design and IT, more and more of this work is being outsourced to freelancers abroad who are able to do the work for much cheaper than in this country. Due to the growth of the internet and the ability to hire 'virtual assistants' even areas such as secretarial work and market research are being outsourced abroad.

Words and Phrases:

Manufacturing.

Outsourcing.

Freelancer(s).

Virtual assistant(s).

Comprehension Questions:

What three sectors are getting smaller?

Where is a lot of the design and IT work being outsourced to?

Answers:

The manufacturing, design and IT sectors are all getting smaller.

A lot of the work is being outsourced abroad.

Part Three

I feel that this country has reached the point where we don't actually make anything anymore. That's a scary position to be in. We used to be a country that manufactured things, that invented, that innovated. But now all we seem to do is serve each other coffee! Don't get me wrong, there is nothing wrong with having a growing service industry, and it does indeed mean that people are spending money. But I'm worried about how they are getting that money. Is it from manufacturing and exporting goods? Is it from having a thriving design industry? Is it from designing and creating cutting-edge technology and software? Or is it just mainly from credit card debt?

We can't just be a nation of consumers. It might be fun for a while but in the end it will go wrong. If we don't want the country to go bankrupt, we need to produce things and then sell them. It's that simple.

Words and Phrases:

Manufacturing

Innovation

Cutting-edge (technology).

Consumer(s).

To be/go bankrupt.

Comprehension Questions:

Does the author think that this country still makes things?

According to the author, what will eventually happen to the country if it doesn't make things and then sell them?

Answers:

No, they don't think that this country still makes things.

They think that the country will go bankrupt.

Is it worth getting a MENTOR?

Part One

When you start a new business enterprise or even if you just become a sole trader, there is a lot to think about. You need a business plan. You need to think about what niche you will enter. You need to think about whether you will take on angel investors, fund it yourself or take a loan from a bank. In fact the amount of things you need to consider can be quite scary.

This is why you should definitely consider getting a mentor. Basically this is someone (usually an entrepreneur themselves) who has had success in the field that you wish to enter. The advantage of getting a mentor is that you will have someone to ask questions to. For example it can often be very difficult to decide how you are going to brand your company. But if you have someone who has already had success, they will be able to not only give you advice on what works, but they may also be able to introduce you to designers etc. They will also be able to offer ideas about what the best marketing strategy might be for your company.

Words and Phrases:

An enterprise.

A sole trader.

A business plan.

A niche.

An angel investor.

A mentor.

An entrepreneur.

A brand. Branding.

Comprehension Questions:

What are three possible ways to fund your new business?

How could a mentor help you 'brand' your company?

Answers:

You could fund your business yourself, get money from an angel investor or get a loan from a bank.

They could give you advice on branding or maybe introduce you to designers etc.

Part Two

So, how do you actually get a <u>mentor</u>? You could just visit various companies and then try to develop a relationship with someone there. But that may be pretty difficult. The easiest way is to just hire someone to <u>mentor</u> or 'coach' you. Even though you may already have too many <u>overheads</u> when getting your business started, this could actually save you money in the long run. So eventually you will get an excellent <u>ROI (return on investment)</u>.

Words and Phrases:

A mentor.

Overheads.

A return on investment (ROI).

Comprehension Question:

What are the two ways you could get a mentor?

Answer:

You could visit companies and build a relationship with someone or you could just hire a mentor.

ENTREPRENEUR TODAY MAGAZINE: INTERVIEW WITH SUSAN HENDRIX. FOUNDER OF 'SOCIAL?MEDIA!!.CO.LUV'

PART ONE

Susan Hendrix is a very unlikely entrepreneur. At 45, after raising 2 children and with no real business experience she went on to found (start) and run one of the most popular agencies for promoting businesses' 'online presence'.

Entrepreneur Today Magazine (ETM): So Susan, can you tell us a little about how you got started in business.

Susan Hendrix (SH): Well, after my children finished their schooling and left home I suddenly found that I had lots of time on my hands. It was around then that I discovered social media. While most of my friends were using it for gossiping and basically wasting time, I saw that there was much more to it than that. I wanted to start teaching a sewing class from my house and didn't know how to get students. So I just mentioned it on my social media pages and within days I had 14 people sign-up for the class. It was amazing.

ETM: So was it then that you decided to start a company helping other companies use social media to promote their businesses?

SH: No, it happened much more gradually than that. At about the same time that I was doing the sewing classes my husband's firm was running a very expensive ad-campaign in order to get new clients. Unfortunately it wasn't going very well and he was really starting to worry. One evening I mentioned how easy it was for me to sign-up clients to my class even though all I did was post some stuff on social media. As nothing else had worked he was willing to give it a try.

ETM: How did it go?

SH: Well it wasn't as easy as with the class. With that, I just told my friends via social media and then they told their friends and so on. But with an actual company it is not that simple. For starters I needed to work out how to reach the people that would be interested in the company's products. I needed to reach the consumer.

ETM: Was the campaign successful?

SH: For the first few months nothing much happened but after a while I really began to master how to use social media and after 6 months it was really starting to work. The company's turnover eventually increased by 20% that year and they had to expand in order to keep up with demand.

Words and Phrases:

Online presence.

Social media.

A firm.

An ad-campaign.

A consumer.

Turnover.

To expand.

Comprehension Questions:

What was the first project she used social media to promote?

Who's company did she first start helping with their online presence?

In her first job how much did turnover increase by?

Answers:

She promoted her sewing class through social media.

She first started helping her husband's company.

Turnover increased by 20%.

Part Two

ETM: Was it then that you decided to start your company?

SH: Actually my husband wanted me to start working for him full time. But I'd always been a bit of a <u>wantrepreneur</u>. I'd always started projects but never really gotten anywhere with them, so I felt that this was my opportunity to really do something. I knew I had the skills to help promote other businesses but I didn't know where to get started.

ETM: So what did you do?

SH: I got my husband to ring all of his business <u>contacts</u> and tell them about the success he had been having by using <u>social media</u> and that they should contact me if they were interested. One company in particular was interested but they were already in talks with another company about improving their <u>online presence</u>. I worked really hard and put together a great <u>bid</u>. Luckily I won the <u>contract</u> and they became my first real clients.

ETM: And what happened then?

SH: Well after a while my reputation grew and I started signing more and more clients. So I started to employ people and it just sort of <u>scaled</u> up from there.

ETM: What type of companies do you mainly deal with now?

SH: Well we have a lot of <u>brick and mortar businesses</u> that use us to help promote their services in their local area. We also work with some <u>manufacturing</u> firms to help them with the online aspect of their <u>product launches</u>.

ETM: What are your plans for the future?

SH: Well we have just started a joint venture with a company that makes apps. We will be making an app so businesses can track all of their social media activity from one place.

ETM: Sounds great, thanks for talking to us today.

SH: No problem, it was a pleasure.

Words and Phrases:

A wantrepreneur.

A contact.

A bid.

A contract.

To scale.

A brick and mortar business.

Manufacturing.

A product launch.

A joint venture.

Comprehension Questions:

How did she get her first real client?

What types of businesses are her main clients?

What type of company are they doing a joint venture with?

Answers:

She got her first real client through her husband's contacts.

Her main clients are 'brick and mortar' businesses and 'manufacturing' companies.

The joint venture is with a company that makes 'apps'.

Start with what you know

If I could give one piece of advice to people who want to start their own company it would be to first get a job in the field you want to start a business in. This is an excellent way to learn all you can about that industry, and make sure that you will be able to enter that market without too much trouble.

This is exactly what I did when I got started. I got a job with one of the biggest producers of software for the television industry (at that time they had a 32% market share), and spent 3 years learning everything I could. During that time I went from being a regular employee to one of the department heads. So I had lots of different experiences there.

I found that being the 'head of a department' was the most useful for learning how to run a company. Not only did I have to delegate to the other employees I was also in charge of helping the tax office when they did an audit of our company. I even had to report to the shareholders sometimes. I was also often sent as a delegate to conferences and had to promote and represent our company.

In that time I was even involved in filing a patent application for some of the technology we had developed. I even worked in the sales department for a while where I was in contact with various software dealers who sold our products to the general public. This was great because I made a lot of contacts in that industry.

After working there for 3 years I felt absolutely confident that I could start my own company, and that's exactly what I did. Now that I have my own company I feel that I already have the experience necessary to make it a success.

Words and Phrases:

A market share.

To delegate.

An audit.

Shareholder(s).

A delegate.

A patent.

A dealer.

A contact.

Comprehension Questions:

How long did the author work at the company?

As a delegate, what did they do?

What was the patent for?

Do they still work at that company?

Answers:

They worked there for 3 years.

As a delegate they represented and promoted the company.

The patent was for technology the company had developed.

No, they now have their own company.

A VICTIM OF SUCCESS?

PART ONE

Is it possible to become too successful too quickly? When we start a new company or become a sole-proprietor of course we want to be as successful as possible, but if it happens too quickly you can sometimes run into trouble. When I started my first company it was during a serious <u>upturn</u> in the economy. People were spending money like crazy and I felt that it would be a great time to start a company. I read a ton of books on starting a business and decided to start off as a company rather than as a <u>sole proprietor</u>. I then started researching various different <u>niches</u> and decided that I would <u>manufacture</u> and sell women's clothing for Yoga and Pilates. Instead of making a whole line of clothing I decided to do a <u>minimum viable product</u> and then go from there. That was a great idea because I quickly discovered that the clothing would *also* be popular with men. So I <u>pivoted</u> my company to be directed towards both sexes.

Words and Phrases:

An upturn (in the economy).

A sole proprietor.

A niche.

To manufacture.

A minimum viable product.

To pivot.

Comprehension Questions:

Was the economy doing well when he first started up in business?

Did he form a company or was he a sole proprietor?

In the end did he only make clothing for women?

Answers:

Yes the economy was doing well.

He formed a company.

No. In the end he made clothing for men and women.

Part Two

When I first got started I wrote a mission statement saying that I wanted to scale the business up as fast as possible. Now, this seemed like a good idea at the time but I had no idea of what problems it would cause. I was pretty good at selling my products and did many transactions each day. But I was terrible at keeping in contact with the manufacturing company and making sure that I always had enough stock to actually sell. Sometimes I'd even have to buy a similar product wholesale and then sell that instead. This was because I didn't have enough of my own product in stock. I was also awful at keeping an eye on cash-flow and was always having to borrow money. I never had any petty cash so I was always using my own money instead of money from the company. So even though we were getting loads of orders and were becoming really popular, because I was trying to do everything so quickly I was actually in danger of completely destroying my own company. Eventually I slowed down, learnt about cash-flow and turned my business into a really successful firm. I learnt that if you want to grow your company, it's best to do it slowly, or you risk going bankrupt.

Words and Phrases:

A mission statement.

A transaction.

A manufacturing (company).

Wholesale.

Cash-flow.

Petty cash.

A firm.

To go/be bankrupt.

Comprehension Questions:

What did they write in their 'mission statement'?

Did they only sell their own products?

Was the problem that they were not getting any orders?

Answers:

In the 'mission statement' they wrote that they would scale the business up as fast as possible.

No. Occasionally they had to sell other products because they ran out of their own product stock.

No. They *were* getting orders. The problem was that they were trying to grow the company too quickly.

Want to Make it Big Online?

Part One

With technology getting better and better, starting an online business has never been easier. But what type of business is best for you, and once you get started what is the best way to promote it? Let's take a look at two excellent online business models.

Ecommerce. This is when you actually sell something online. This can be a real item that you ship to your customers by post such as clothing or DVDs. You can also use ecommerce to sell digital downloads such as eBooks and music.

Passive Income. Passive income is money you make when you are not actually working. For example if you have a blog or a forum and then place pay per click advertising on it, you will make money every time someone clicks on it.

Words and Phrases:

Ecommerce.

Digital downloads.

eBooks.

Passive Income.

A forum.

Pay per click (advertising).

Comprehension Questions:

With ecommerce, can you only sell goods that you have to ship to the customer?

What are two examples of digital downloads?

What is passive income?

Answers:

No. You can also sell digital downloads.

eBooks and music are two examples of digital downloads.

Passive income is money that you earn when you are not actually working.

Part Two

Whatever online business model you choose, you will have to get people to visit your website. If you want to expand your online presence and get more organic traffic to your site you definitely need to learn about SEO. This is basically when you make your website as easy to find on the internet as possible. This includes things like adding keywords to your text and making sure that your SERP result is well written and attractive to customers. If you want to track your progress, be sure to install website analytics onto your site. This is a way for you to track how many people visit your site and what pages they visit the most. Whatever you do, make sure that you use white hat and not black hat SEO tactics. This is because search engines such as Google, don't like 'black hat' tactics and will make your site difficult to find if they catch you using these methods.

Once you have decided what type of online business you want and then get some visitors to your site, you then need to convert them into customers. A great way to do this is to learn copywriting. This is when you write in a way that makes people want to buy things.

Whatever path you decide to take, just remember that persistence is key. If something's not working just keep pivoting until you find something that works.

Words and Phrases:

An online presence.

Organic traffic.

SEO (Search Engine Optimization).

Website analytics.

White hat/black hat (SEO tactics).

To convert. A conversion.

To pivot.

Comprehension Questions:

What is a good way to get more organic traffic to your website?

Which is better, 'white hat' or 'black hat' SEO tactics?

What is 'copywriting'?

Answers:

Learning about SEO is a good way to get organic traffic to your website.

'White hat' SEO tactics are better than 'black hat' ones.

Copywriting is when you write in a way that makes people want to buy things.

DIFFERENT INVESTING TECHNIQUES FOR DIFFERENT MARKET CONDITIONS?

PART ONE

Is it necessary to alter the way you choose stocks depending on whether it's a <u>bull or a bear market</u>? For example if you usually follow '<u>value investing</u>' methods, will that work in a <u>bear market</u> when most of the stocks are going down in value? What I mean is that during a <u>bear market</u> it is usual for most of the stocks to go down in value, even if they are actually great companies. So even if you've done loads of research and are sure that the stock is great 'value' you could still end up losing money.

Words and Phrases:

A bull market. A bear market.

Value investing.

Comprehension Question:

Do most stocks go down in value during a bear market?

Answer:

Yes. Most stocks go down in value during a bear market.

Part Two

On the other hand, if you follow 'trends' it doesn't matter if the company is good or not. All you are doing is noting which direction the stock is 'trending' in and then either going long (if the price is rising) or shorting it (if the price is going down). Some say that this type of 'investing' is not real investing at all but is just speculation. But isn't all investing a type of speculation? Even if you mainly invest to get paid dividends, you are still 'speculating' that the price of the stock will go up.

The opposite of following trends is to be a 'contrarian investor'. This is when you do the opposite of what everybody else is doing. This is based on the idea that 'crowds of people' often do crazy things, so it's best to go against them and do you own thing.

Words and Phrases:

Trend (following).

Going long (on a stock).

To short (a stock).

Speculation.

Dividends.

Contrarian investing. A contrarian investor.

Comprehension Questions:

With trend following, does it matter if the stock is good or not?

If a stock is going down in value, how can you make money from it?

What do contrarian investors do?

Answers:

No it doesn't matter if the stock is good or not.

You can make money from a stock going down in value by 'shorting' it.

Contrarian investors do the opposite of what everybody else is doing.

Part Three

Some might say that the best thing to do is to <u>diversify</u> within your <u>stock portfolio</u>. But you will still be affected in a <u>bear market</u>. Even if you <u>take a position</u> in lots of different stocks, if most stocks are going down in value you will still be hit. You could try '<u>dollar cost averaging</u>' which is when you buy stocks regularly over a long period of time. This means that even if the price goes up or down you will still get the average price in the long run.

Like most things in life, it's probably best to take the best from each technique and then just do what works best for you.

Words and Phrases:

Diversification.

A stock portfolio.

(To take) a position (in a stock).

Dollar cost averaging.

Comprehension Questions:

If you diversify your stock portfolio, will you be safe in a bear market?

What is a good way to get the 'average' price when buying stocks?

Answers:

No. You may still take a hit if all of the stocks go down in value.

Dollar cost averaging is a good way to get the 'average' price of a stock.

Honesty About a Broken System?

This week a video has gone viral of a broker (who was filmed without his knowledge) speaking about some of the common practices at his investment bank. The video has caused a lot of shock as he openly talks about some of the illegal practices that employees of the bank often do. It has caused particular anger as many people feel that, as this bank was bailed out during the financial crisis, the government should be keeping a closer watch on them.

In the first part of the video, he discusses the fact that insider trading during IPOs is common and that brokers also often front run their client's deals. He also talks about how some of the brokers were selling their clients a certain stock even though they knew there was probably a lot of downside to it. That would have been ok if they had explained that there was a risk that the stock could go lower in price and that they should probably put a 'stop' in place. But they didn't do that, in fact they did the opposite and said that there was so much upside that it would keep going up in price. In fact it did go up a bit in price but then hit a ceiling and went dropping down. If the brokers had at least put a limit order on it they would have made their clients some money, but they didn't even do that. Needless to say the stock dropped and a lot of people lost a lot of money. It eventually found a floor at about half the price of what the initial investors had paid.

Even though a lot of what he talks about is just immoral, there are also many criminal acts he describes as well. But will the government take action? We will have to wait and see.

Words and Phrases:

A viral video.

A broker.

A bail out.

Insider trading.

IPO (Initial Public Offering).

Front running.

Downside (to a stock).

A stop.

Upside (to a stock).

A ceiling (to a stock).

A limit order.

A floor (to a stock).

Comprehension Questions:

Is there insider trading during some IPOs?

Are the brokers properly warning their clients of the risks of some stocks?

With the stock mentioned in the article, did the brokers place a 'stop' on it?

Answers:

Yes there is insider trading during some IPOs.

No they are not warning their clients of the risks.

No they did not place 'stops' on the stock.

Thank you for reading!

Keep reviewing and using your new vocabulary and you will sound fluent in no time.

Please remember to review this book. I am a small publisher and rely on word of mouth to reach new students.

Good luck on your journey to English fluency.

www.ingramcontent.com/pod-product-compliance
Lightning Source LLC
Chambersburg PA
CBHW072054110526
44590CB00018B/3172